Editors
Janet Cain, M.Ed.
Mara Ellen Guckian

Managing Editor
Ina Massler Levin, M.A.

Editor-in-Chief
Sharon Coan, M.S. Ed.

Cover Artist
Denice Adorno

Illustrator
Howard Chaney

Art Coordinator
Denice Adorno

Product Manager
Phil Garcia

Imaging
Rosa C. See

Publishers
Rachelle Cracchiolo, M.S. Ed.
Mary Dupuy Smith, M.S. Ed.

U.S. History Brain Teasers
USA

Author
Cynthia Holzschuher, M.Ed.

Teacher Created Materials, Inc.
6421 Industry Way
Westminster, CA 92683
www.teachercreated.com
© 2001 Teacher Created Materials, Inc.
Made in U.S.A.
ISBN-1-57690-639-6

The classroom teacher may reproduce copies of materials in this book for classroom use only. The reproduction of any part for an entire school or school system is strictly prohibited. No part of this publication may be transmitted, stored, or recorded in any form without written permission from the publisher.

TABLE OF CONTENTS

Introduction 2

Early Explorations 3

Native Americans 10

Foundation of a New Country 14

Emancipation and Reconstruction 33

World Conflict in a New Century 43

Establishment of a Modern Society 52

General Knowledge 66

Answer Key 76

INTRODUCTION

The *Brain Teasers* series provides ways to exercise and develop brain power! Each page stands alone and can be used as a quick and easy filler activity. The pages can be distributed to students as individual worksheets or made into transparencies for presentation to the entire class. The activities are especially useful in helping students develop:

- logic and other critical thinking skills
- creative thinking skills
- research skills
- spelling and vocabulary skills
- general knowledge skills

This *United States History Brain Teasers* book can be used in conjunction with a United States social studies curriculum to reinforce learning. The most current data has been used in this book as much as possible.

To make some of the puzzles more difficult, you may wish to block out or fold under word banks before duplicating the pages.

Allow students to use a variety of reference books or the World Wide Web to complete some or all of the activities. We hope you and your students will have great fun learning more about the people and events that shaped our country's history.

Early Explorations

COMING TO AMERICA

European immigrants came to this country for many reasons. Most hoped to find a better way of life. Sort these foreign language words to their correct meaning in English. You may wish to use this Web site for help: *http://babelfish.altavista.digital.com/*

welcome	
French	
German	
Spanish	

America	
French	
German	
Spanish	

freedom	
French	
German	
Spanish	

immigrant	
French	
German	
Spanish	

democracy	
French	
German	
Spanish	

Word Bank

bienvenido	der Einwanderer	democrácia
Amérique	immigré	immigrante
die Freiheit	libertad	América
liberté	democratie	bienvenue
willkommen	Amerika	die Demokratie

© Teacher Created Materials, Inc.   #2639 U. S. History Brain Teasers

Early Explorations

GEOGRAPHY WORD PAIRS

The first definition in each pair is for a geography word. Fill in the blanks to spell the word. Change one letter in the geography word to spell the word that fits the second definition.

1. opposite of north S o u t h
   used to eat and speak m o u t h

2. inland body of water l a k e
   narrow passageway l a n e

3. 5,280 feet (1609 m) ___ ___ ___ ___
   pack animal ___ ___ ___ ___

4. investigate ___ ___ ___ ___ ___ ___ ___
   to burst noisily ___ ___ ___ ___ ___ ___

5. flat drawing of land ___ ___ ___
   head covering ___ ___ ___

6. opposite of east ___ ___ ___ ___
   good, better, ___ ___ ___ ___

7. ground ___ ___ ___ ___
   body part ___ ___ ___ ___

8. large body of saltwater ___ ___ ___
   beverage ___ ___ ___

9. peak ___ ___ ___ ___ ___ ___ ___ ___
   source of water for drinking ___ ___ ___ ___ ___ ___ ___ ___

10. end of Earth's axis ___ ___ ___ ___
    pit in the ground ___ ___ ___ ___

11. sovereign republic ___ ___ ___ ___ ___
    rock or writing surface ___ ___ ___ ___ ___

12. border ___ ___ ___ ___ ___
    green citrus fruit ___ ___ ___ ___ ___

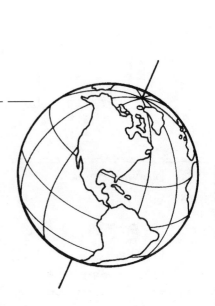

#2639 U. S. History Brain Teasers   4   © Teacher Created Materials, Inc.

Early Explorations

GEOGRAPHY TERMS

Draw a line through ten words hidden in this puzzle. Circle the letters in between the words and print them on the lines at the bottom of the box to find out how the words are alike. Then answer the riddle.

```
H A R B O R G E G L A C I E R O
M O U N T A I N G R V A L L E Y
A D E S E R T P H R I V E R I C
I S L A N D T E V O L C A N O S
P R A I R I E R O C E A N S M S
```

_ _ _ _ _ _ _ _ _ _ _ _ _ _ _ _

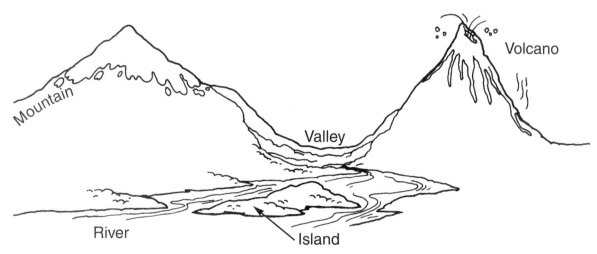

Riddle: How is an island the opposite of a lake?

_____

_____

Early Explorations

HISTORY HOMOPHONES

Read each word. Write a word that sounds the same but is spelled differently on the line next to each word. The words you write will relate to the settling of America.

1. piece _____
2. seas _____
3. plane _____
4. sale _____
5. whirled _____
6. heard _____
7. sight _____
8. hoarse _____
9. straight _____
10. billed _____

11. fur _____
12. pour _____
13. rain _____
14. tacks _____
15. capital _____
16. seed _____
17. core _____
18. root _____
19. thrown _____
20. wore _____

#2639 U. S. History Brain Teasers   6   © Teacher Created Materials, Inc.

Early Explorations

NEW WORLD CHANGES

Here is a list of words that you might read as you learn about life in the New World. Make a new word by changing one vowel (*a, e, i, o, u,* or *y*) in each word to a different vowel. Write the new words on the lines below each word.

1. track

2. master

3. story

4. land

5. map

6. leader

7. farm

8. sea

9. battle

10. born

11. rule

12. ruin

13. paddle

14. trap

15. shoot

Early Explorations

TRADITIONAL FOODS

Six families emigrated to the United States from different countries. Read the statements about the foods these families like to eat that remind them of their homelands. Mark an **X** in the box that tells where each family lived before coming to America.

	Ireland	Russia	Italy	Germany	Mexico	China
Kim's Family						
Pietro's Family						
Sofia's Family						
Rosita's Family						
Sean's Family						
Hans's Family						

1. Kim's family likes to eat stir-fried vegetables and rice.

2. Pietro's family enjoys cabbage cooked in a thick soup with beets and other vegetables.

3. Sofia's family cooks tomatoes to make a spicy sauce for pasta.

4. Rosita's family uses fresh, chopped tomatoes and chili peppers in a spicy hot sauce for tacos.

5. Sean's family eats potatoes at nearly every meal.

6. Hans's family loves sausage and sauerkraut, which is a tangy cabbage.

Early Explorations

EUROPEANS EXPLORE A NEW LAND

Europeans came to the New World seeking fame and fortune. They risked a dangerous sea voyage to win the favor of their king or queen. Make as many different words as you can from the following words. Be sure to keep the letters in the order they appear in the given word or words. Do not include one-letter words.

Example: FRONTIER   front,   on,   tie,   tier

1. JACQUES CARTIER

   ___ ___   _____   ___   ____   ____

2. NORTHWEST PASSAGE

   __ ___   _____   ___   ___

   ____   ____   ___

3. CHAMPLAIN

   _____   ____   __   _____

   ____   ___

4. FRANCISCO CORONADO

   ___   __   _____   ___   ____

5. FRANCIS DRAKE

   ___   __   ____   ____

6. CHRISTOPHER COLUMBUS

   __   ____   ___   _____   ___

   ___   ___

7. SPANISH ARMADA

   ____   ____   ____   ____

   ___   __

8. SCANDINAVIA

   ____   ___   ___   ____

9. EUROPEAN

   ____

10. NETHERLANDS

    ___   ____   ___   ____   _____

© Teacher Created Materials, Inc.   9   #2639 U. S. History Brain Teasers

Native Americans

NATIVE AMERICAN LIFE

Settlers who came to America saw that Native Americans respected the environment and tried to live in harmony with nature. Native Americans believed that the land was made for all people and that it should be shared. Use the answers in the circles to fill in the blanks. Cross off each answer as you use it. The answer that is left in the circles will complete the bonus sentence.

1. Shelter made of buffalo hide _____
2. Common weapon used by hunters and warriors _____
3. Shiny items purchased from European traders _____
4. Nature's greatest gift to the Indians _____
5. Groups of Indians who followed the herds of buffalo _____
6. Form of communication _____
7. Animal used for shelter, clothing, and food _____
8. Animal used for transportation _____
9. Iroquois home _____
10. Steep, flat-topped mountain _____
11. Fish preserved by drying and smoking _____
12. Foot covering made of moose hide _____
13. Indian name for corn _____
14. Indian ceremony to celebrate wealth _____
15. Crop other than corn _____

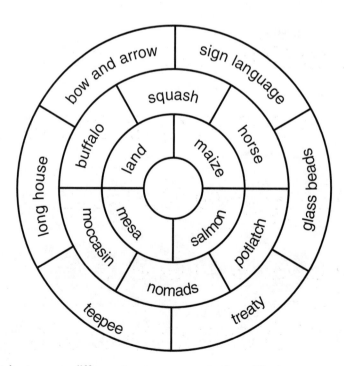

Bonus: An agreement between different governments is called a _____.

#2639 U. S. History Brain Teasers 10 © Teacher Created Materials, Inc.

Native Americans

CULTURE GROUPS

The customs, religious beliefs, and traditions of Native American culture groups differed depending on their location and ancestry. Early settlers found many groups of Native Americans living together in the New World. Color some of the letters from each line to name a group of Native Americans. The name of the group will always start with the first letter in each line. After coloring the circles, write the name of the Native American group on the lines.

1. Ⓟ Ⓣ Ⓡ Ⓤ Ⓨ Ⓔ Ⓔ Ⓣ Ⓥ Ⓑ Ⓡ Ⓦ Ⓛ Ⓜ Ⓟ Ⓞ
   P U E B L O

2. Ⓐ Ⓕ Ⓡ Ⓔ Ⓡ Ⓐ Ⓤ Ⓟ Ⓞ Ⓓ Ⓐ Ⓖ Ⓗ Ⓔ Ⓣ Ⓞ
   A R A P A H O

3. Ⓒ Ⓑ Ⓞ Ⓡ Ⓜ Ⓘ Ⓐ Ⓨ Ⓝ Ⓠ Ⓒ Ⓚ Ⓗ Ⓘ Ⓔ
   C O M A N C H E

4. Ⓒ Ⓑ Ⓗ Ⓡ Ⓣ Ⓔ Ⓤ Ⓨ Ⓣ Ⓡ Ⓔ Ⓜ Ⓝ Ⓞ Ⓟ Ⓝ Ⓡ Ⓔ
   C H E Y E N N E

5. Ⓟ Ⓞ Ⓞ Ⓐ Ⓟ Ⓟ Ⓦ Ⓒ Ⓒ Ⓝ Ⓣ Ⓣ Ⓔ Ⓗ Ⓗ Ⓔ
   P A W N E E

6. Ⓐ Ⓦ Ⓟ Ⓡ Ⓔ Ⓐ Ⓨ Ⓒ Ⓘ Ⓝ Ⓗ Ⓡ Ⓔ
   A P A C H E

7. Ⓒ Ⓑ Ⓓ Ⓡ Ⓤ Ⓤ Ⓘ Ⓞ Ⓣ Ⓨ Ⓦ Ⓞ Ⓟ Ⓡ
   C R O W

8. Ⓢ Ⓣ Ⓘ Ⓞ Ⓟ Ⓡ Ⓞ Ⓝ Ⓤ Ⓡ Ⓦ Ⓥ Ⓧ
   S I O U X

9. Ⓞ Ⓤ Ⓢ Ⓞ Ⓟ Ⓐ Ⓞ Ⓓ Ⓖ Ⓜ Ⓣ Ⓔ
   O S A G E

10. Ⓒ Ⓙ Ⓡ Ⓞ Ⓟ Ⓡ Ⓔ Ⓒ Ⓔ Ⓜ Ⓨ Ⓙ Ⓚ
    C R E E K

© Teacher Created Materials, Inc.

Native Americans

WORD CLUES

Use the letters in NATIVE AMERICANS to spell the words for these clues. Have fun with this puzzle.

1. ___ ___ ___ ___ = plural of mouse
2. ___ ___ ___ ___ = precipitation
3. ___ ___ ___ ___ = animal flesh
4. ___ ___ ___ ___ ___ = railroad
5. ___ ___ ___ = light brown
6. ___ ___ ___ ___ = cereal grain
7. ___ ___ ___ ___ = told on a clock face
8. ___ ___ ___ ___ = climbing plant
9. ___ ___ ___ ___ = personal identification
10. ___ ___ ___ = not a woman
11. ___ ___ ___ ___ = kind
12. ___ ___ ___ = used for hearing
13. ___ ___ ___ = upper body part
14. ___ ___ ___ ___ = carries blood
15. ___ ___ ___ ___ = most important, primary
16. ___ ___ ___ = metal container
17. ___ ___ ___ ___ = to rip or pull apart
18. ___ ___ ___ = automobile
19. ___ ___ ___ ___ = not messy
20. ___ ___ ___ ___ ___ ___ = for sure, definite

#2639 U. S. History Brain Teasers   12   © Teacher Created Materials, Inc.

Native Americans

PICTURE MEMORY

Look at the pictures of some items that were important in the daily lives of Native Americans. Study the pictures for three minutes. Then put it out of sight. On another sheet of paper, list as many items from the picture as you can remember.

© Teacher Created Materials, Inc.

Foundation of a New Country

COLONIAL RHYMES

Settlers had many challenges facing them in America. They needed food, shelter, and clothing. They needed to make friends with the Native Americans living in the area. Colonial life was often difficult and dangerous. Draw a line to match each phrase to the pair of rhyming words that describes it.

1. to raise wooly animals — crop shop

2. to grow corn — church search

3. a healthy vegetable — plains trains

4. hornbook — raise maize

5. place to buy grain — keep sheep

6. baked salmon — grand land

7. ocean voyage — school tool

8. wonderful country — ship trip

9. groups of Conestoga wagons — green bean

10. to choose where you practice your religion — fish dish

Foundation of a New Country

EARLY AMERICAN ANAGRAMS

Rearrange the letters in these words to find the names of famous Americans. They may be former presidents, colonial leaders, or signers of the Declaration of Independence. The boldfaced letters are the initials of the person's first or last name.

1. SO SEA JAM **M**IND   _ _ _ _ _   _ _ _ _ _ _ _

2. A**N** THAN **H**EAL   _ _ _ _ _ _ _   _ _ _ _

3. JAR INN **F**IN ELM **B**ANK   _ _ _ _ _ _ _ _   _ _ _ _ _ _ _ _

4. OF **J**AM HEN FORE**S**TS   _ _ _ _ _ _ _   _ _ _ _ _ _ _ _ _

5. TOWN HO**G**S A**G**REEING   _ _ _ _ _ _   _ _ _ _ _ _ _ _ _ _

6. A**S** AM MUD SE**A**L   _ _ _ _ _ _   _ _ _ _ _ _

7. **P**URE **R**ELVEA   _ _ _ _   _ _ _ _ _ _

8. MAN **H**ELD RELAX**A**TION   _ _ _ _ _ _ _ _ _ _   _ _ _ _ _ _ _ _

9. ME HA**T** **P**IANOS   _ _ _ _ _ _   _ _ _ _ _

10. SON HAD **J**AM   _ _ _ _ _   _ _ _ _ _ _

11. **H**EN ALL NE**A**T   _ _ _ _ _ _   _ _ _ _ _ _

12. **J**AM NOSE **M**ORE   _ _ _ _ _   _ _ _ _ _ _ _

To make this puzzle more challenging, fold over along the dashed line before reproducing.

John Adams	Nathan Hale	James Monroe
Samuel Adams	Alexander Hamilton	Thomas Paine
Ethan Allen	Thomas Jefferson	Paul Revere
Benjamin Franklin	James Madison	George Washington

© Teacher Created Materials, Inc.   15   #2639 U. S. History Brain Teasers

Foundation of a New Country

THIRTEEN ORIGINAL COLONIES

After the Seven Years' War, colonists no longer wanted the British to control or protect them. It took yet another war, the American Revolution, for the colonists to win their independence. Draw a line through the names of twelve colonies in the puzzle. Circle the letters between each of those names. Print the circled letters on the lines to reveal the name of the thirteenth colony.

```
V I R G I N I A P M A S
S A C H U S E T T S E N
E W H A M P S H I R E N
N E W Y O R K N C O N N
E C T I C U T S M A R Y
L A N D Y R H O D E I S
L A N D L D E L A W A R
E V N O R T H C A R O L
I N A A N E W J E R S E
Y N S O U T H C A R O L
I N A I G E O R G I A A
```

_____ _____ _____ _____ _____ _____ _____ _____ _____ _____ _____

#2639 U. S. History Brain Teasers

Foundation of a New Country

COLONIAL HIDDEN MEANINGS

Find the meanings of these puzzles that relate to colonial life.

Example: | col / eee | col   on   ies = colonies

1. su PEN la _____	2. iVIRGa _____	3. 13 A ORIG L col/eee _____ _____

4. RIVER
 	
L _____
I _____
A _____
S
	5. thewil*lost*derness
	
	_____
	_____
	_____
		6. d s→e
		   a campfire
		  e t a
		
		_____
		_____
		_____
		_____

7. roWwsAofLcoKrn _____ _____ _____	8. Puri 10 10 10 _____	9. thecabinwoods _____ _____ _____

© Teacher Created Materials, Inc. 17 #2639 U. S. History Brain Teasers

Foundation of a New Country

CATEGORIZE FAVORITE THINGS

Colonial children used some words that are no longer used today. The words described many of their favorite foods, clothes, toys, and activities. Write each word from the Word Box under the correct heading of the Categories.

Word Box

spinet	scotch hopping	primer	minuet	stilts
checks	hornbook	muff	tricorne	clogs
jig	breeches	trifle	porridge	cobbler
shepherd's pie	cipher	reel	quill	quoits

Categories

Music/Dance

1. _____ 3. _____

2. _____ 4. _____

Food

1. _____ 3. _____

2. _____ 4. _____

School

1. _____ 3. _____

2. _____ 4. _____

Games/Toys

1. _____ 3. _____

2. _____ 4. _____

Clothing

1. _____ 3. _____

2. _____ 4. _____

Foundation of a New Country

PILGRIMS REBUS

Decode the picture and letter clues to reveal words that are related to the lives of Pilgrims in America..

1. _____   [foot] − e + [neck] − k + co

2. _____   [shell] − l + ter

3. _____   [fire] [arm] + s

4. _____   har + [vest]

5. _____ _____   s + [pear] [fish] + ing

6. _____ _____   [log] [car] + in

7. _____   [can] + dle

8. _____   [pump] + kin

9. _____   [car] + [sack] + e

10. _____   [pot] + a + [toe]

Foundation of a New Country

PATRICK HENRY

Patrick Henry was a great speaker and a delegate to the First Continental Congress. Beginning with the first G, circle every third letter in the grid below to find out how Patrick Henry expressed his feelings about the colonists' struggle for independence from British rule. Write this famous statement on the lines.

```
Ⓖ U E I T L V R S E J O M R W E I P L
O P I G T B R E E G U R O K T B U Y U I
O P Y R M K G R W I G F V R E E M M
M H Y E H Y D O U E B Y A P Y T L M H
```

" __ __ __ __ __ __ __ __ __ __ __ __ __ __ __, __ __
 __ __ __ __ __ __ __ __ __ __ __ __ __!"

Use a reference book to answer these questions about Patrick Henry. Circle the correct word to complete each sentence.

1. Patrick Henry was a (lawyer, policeman).

2. He lived in (Tennessee, Virginia).

3. He was against the (Stamp Act, Erie Canal).

4. Patrick Henry challenged the colonists to fight for (peace, freedom).

5. Patrick Henry was a gifted (actor, orator).

#2639 U. S. History Brain Teasers

Foundation of a New Country

BOSTON TEA PARTY

American colonists who were dressed as Native Americans took only three hours to dump 90,000 pounds of tea into the Boston Harbor. They did not want to pay the tax on tea to the British government. When the British tried to close Boston Harbor, the First Continental Congress responded by cutting off all trade with Britain.

Use the clues to identify words that relate to the Boston Tea Party.

1. Nickname for the British troops

2. British governmental body

3. British tea exporter

4. Colonists protested taxation without this.

5. These groups shared news among the colonies.

6. Organized refusal to buy a product or service

7. This group of colonists dumped the tea.

8. This man led the group that dumped the tea.

9. Acts that closed the British Harbor to almost all shipping and trade

10. Tax based on the amount of money earned

11. Tax based on the price of goods and paid at the time of purchase

Foundation of a New Country

CONSTITUTIONALLY CORRECT

On September 17, 1787, the Constitution of the United States was read in Philadelphia, Pennsylvania. It took two years for all thirteen states to approve this plan for governing their new nation. The first ten amendments, ratified on June 8, 1789, are called the Bill of Rights. On the lines, write the number of the amendment described. Then add or subtract the numbers as indicated to find the final answer.

_____ Repealed prohibition

+ _____ Limited the president to two terms

+ _____ Gave women the right to vote

− _____ Outlined the plan for replacing the president in case of his inability to serve

+ _____ Outlawed the poll tax

− _____ Gave Washington, D.C., residents the right to vote for president

+ _____ Outlawed the making or drinking of alcoholic beverages

+ _____ Changed the date of the presidential inauguration to January 20

− _____ Lowered the voting age to 18

= _____ Total number of states in the United States today

Foundation of a New Country

STAR-SPANGLED BANNER

The words to the "Star-Spangled Banner" were written in 1814 by Francis Scott Key as he watched the bombardment of Fort McHenry. They were set to the tune of an English drinking song. On March 3, 1931, President Herbert Hoover signed a bill that made the song the national anthem of the United States. Can you fill in the missing words in the first verse of the "Star-Spangled Banner"?

"O! SAY, CAN YOU _____, BY THE _____ EARLY LIGHT,

WHAT SO PROUDLY WE _____ AT THE _____ LAST GLEAMING.

WHOSE BROAD _____ AND BRIGHT _____, THROUGH THE

_____ FIGHT,

O'ER THE _____ WE WATCHED WERE SO GALLANTLY _____?

AND THE _____ RED GLARE, THE _____ BURSTING IN AIR,

GAVE _____ THROUGH THE NIGHT THAT OUR _____ WAS STILL THERE.

O! SAY DOES THAT _____ SPANGLED BANNER YET WAVE

O'ER THE _____ OF THE FREE AND THE _____ OF THE BRAVE?"

Use a reference book to identify the years for these former United States flags.

1. _____
Continental Colors

2. _____
First Stars and Stripes

3. _____
26-star flag

4. _____
30-star flag

5. _____
36-star flag

6. _____
48-star flag

© Teacher Created Materials, Inc. #2639 U. S. History Brain Teasers

Foundation of a New Country

THE AMERICAN REVOLUTION

People in the thirteen colonies united to fight against the well-trained British army. General George Washington led the Continental Army into many battles against the British. Use the clues to complete the crossword puzzle.

Across

1. George _____ led the Continental Army.
3. British troops surrendered at _____.
5. Part-time colonial soldiers were called _____.
7. Nickname for British troops _____
9. Thomas _____ was the author of *Common Sense*.
10. Paul _____ was a silversmith.

Down

2. The first shots of the American Revolution were fired at _____ and Concord.
4. Colonists fought to win their _____.
6. British monarch, _____ George
8. The_____ of Paris ended the war.

#2639 U. S. History Brain Teasers 24 © Teacher Created Materials, Inc.

Foundation of a New Country

SURFIN' THE COLONIES

The imaginary Internet addresses listed below use the nicknames of the states that once were the original thirteen colonies. On each line, write the name of the state to which the address belongs.

1. www.granitestate.com _____

2. www.bakedbeansstate.com _____

3. www.empirestate.com _____

4. www.littlerhody.com _____

5. www.landofsteadyinhabitants.com _____

6. www.gardenstate.com _____

7. www.firststate.com _____

8. www.freestate.com _____

9. www.motherofpresidents.com _____

10. www.tarheelstate.com _____

11. www.ricestate.com _____

12. www.gooberstate.com _____

13. www.keystonestate.com _____

On the lines below, write the names of the first three colonies to become states and the dates they joined the Union.

1. _____ _____

2. _____ _____

3. _____ _____

Foundation of a New Country

SPLIT PROVERBS

Benjamin Franklin began printing *Poor Richard's Almanac* in 1733. The little book contained many clever sayings that offered good advice for successful living. Many of these sayings are still quoted today. Complete these proverbs with phrases from the box.

1. Have you something to do tomorrow, _____.
2. A true friend is _____.
3. No gain, _____.
4. Be always ashamed to _____.
5. People who are wrapped up in themselves make _____.
6. A penny saved is _____.
7. Early to bed and early to rise, makes a man _____.
8. 'Tis easier to prevent bad habits than _____.
9. An ounce of prevention is worth _____.
10. A bird in the hand is worth _____.

```
a penny earned

two in the bush

catch thyself idle

the best possession

a pound of cure

healthy, wealthy, and wise

without pain

to break them

small packages

do it today
```

Foundation of a New Country

READ ALL ABOUT IT!

The following historic events occurred between 1780 and 1850. Fill in the dates to show when you would have seen these headlines in the newspaper. Use a reference book to help you.

1. Gold Discovered at Sutter's Mill _____

2. Texans Defend Alamo to Their Deaths _____

3. Erie Canal Completed _____

4. Lewis and Clark Set Off to Explore Louisiana Territory _____

5. George Washington Becomes Country's First President _____

6. Nine States Ratify Constitution _____

7. Thomas Jefferson Elected President _____

8. British Ships Pound Fort McHenry _____

9. Cornwallis Surrenders at Yorktown _____

10. Convention Writes New Plan for Government _____

11. Old Ironsides Survives British Attack _____

12. Washington Lawyer Pens National Song _____

Foundation of a New Country

QUOTABLE QUOTES

Circle the name of the famous American who made each statement.

---

1. "Give me liberty, or give me death!"

    Patrick Henry　　　　George Washington　　　　Benjamin Franklin

2. "I only regret that I have but one life to lose for my country."

    Patrick Henry　　　　George Washington　　　　Nathan Hale

3. "My paramount object in this struggle is to save the Union, and is not either to save or destroy slavery."

    George Washington　　　　Abraham Lincoln　　　　Benjamin Franklin

4. "Liberty, when it begins to take root, is a plant rapid in growth."

    Abraham Lincoln　　　　Benjamin Franklin　　　　George Washington

5. "All would live long, but none would be old."

    Abraham Lincoln　　　　Benjamin Franklin　　　　George Washington

6. "We must indeed all hang together, or most assuredly, we shall hang separately."

    Patrick Henry　　　　George Washington　　　　Benjamin Franklin

7. "In giving freedom to the slave, we assure freedom to the free."

    Frederick Douglass　　　　Abraham Lincoln　　　　Sojourner Truth

8. "War begins where reason ends."

    Frederick Douglass　　　　Abraham Lincoln　　　　Sojourner Truth

9. "I could work as much as a man . . . and ain't I a woman?"

    Sojourner Truth　　　　Harriet Tubman　　　　Louisa May Alcott

10. "No man who ever held the office of president would ever congratulate a friend on obtaining it."

    John Adams　　　　George Washington　　　　Abraham Lincoln

Foundation of a New Country

IMPORTANT TREATY

In 1803 the French controlled much of the land in what is now our nation. The United States sent a representative to Paris, France, to negotiate the purchase of the great territory the French owned. Answer the five basic reporter's questions to tell about this event.

Who from the United States was involved in the purchase?
_____

What was the name of this historic event?
_____

When was this historic purchase made?
_____

Where was this territory located?
_____

How much land was bought, and how much did it cost?
_____

List the thirteen states that were later formed from this land.

1. _____
2. _____
3. _____
4. _____
5. _____
6. _____
7. _____
8. _____
9. _____
10. _____
11. _____
12. _____
13. _____

Foundation of a New Country

MISSISSPPI RIVER GEOGRAPHY

The Mississippi River is one of the world's greatest rivers, and it is the longest river in the United States. It provides a natural habitat for a wide variety of birds and animals. On the map, label the states that are touched by the mighty Mississippi. Then, on the lines provided, label these cities: St. Louis, New Orleans, Memphis, Minneapolis, Cairo, and Natchez.

Foundation of a New Country

WOMEN'S RIGHTS

Women officially began their organized struggle for equal rights at the Women's Rights Convention in Seneca Falls, New York, in 1848. This courageous gathering inspired other women and men to work for women's rights. Match these women to their main contribution toward changing society. Write the correct names on the lines.

> Jane Addams   Susan B. Anthony
> Lucretia Mott   Margaret Sanger
> Carry Nation   Harriet Beecher Stowe
> Elizabeth Cady Stanton Sojourner Truth
> Jeannette Rankin   Harriet Tubman

1. Made the nation understand the horrors of slavery by writing *Uncle Tom's Cabin*

2. Social reformer who founded Hull House to help the poor

3. Two women who organized the Women's Rights Convention at Seneca Falls, New York

4. Freed slave who became an abolitionist and feminist

5. Temperance reformer who destroyed saloons during prohibition

6. Was a nurse who cared for the poor in New York City and then became an author

7. First woman to cast a vote in the United States, even though it was illegal

8. Escaped slave who became a famous conductor on the Underground Railroad

9. Feminist and legislator

© Teacher Created Materials, Inc.   31   #2639 U. S. History Brain Teasers

Foundation of a New Country

SETTLING THE WEST

Write the letter of the description on the line before the clues that match it.

____ 1. Meriwether Lewis, William Clark, Zebullon Pike

____ 2. Missouri, Arkansas, Louisiana

____ 3. California, Sutter's Mill, Sacramento

____ 4. steamboats, covered wagons, railroad

____ 5. Arkansas, Red, Missouri

____ 6. England, France, Spain

____ 7. Rocky, Smoky, Appalachian

____ 8. Thomas Jefferson, John Hancock, Benjamin Franklin

____ 9. Oregon, Santa Fe, Old Spanish

____10. Cheyenne, Sioux, Pawnee

____11. steel plow, barbed wire, windmill

____12. territory, acre, state

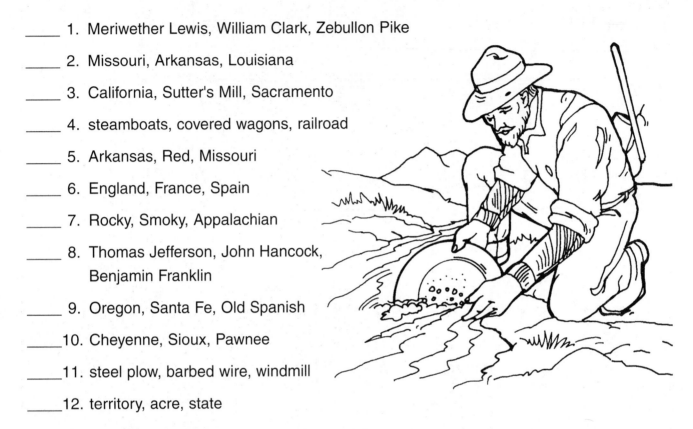

a. divisions of land in the territories

b. signers of the Declaration of Independence

c. groups of Native Americans who lived on the plains

d. early explorers

e. foreign countries that owned American land

f. inventions that helped settlers

g. rivers west of the Mississippi River

h. Gold Rush locations

i. trails in the Old West

j. places west of the Mississippi River

k. transportation

l. names of American mountain ranges

Emancipation and Reconstruction

ABRAHAM LINCOLN TIME LINE

Abraham Lincoln was born February 12, 1809, in Hardin County, Kentucky. He moved with his parents to Illinois and attended school while working on a farm, splitting rails for fences, and clerking in a store. He spent eight years in the Illinois legislature, where he rode the circuit of courts for many years. Write the event from the box next to the correct date below.

- wins election to House of Representatives
- marries Mary Todd
- becomes 16th president of the United States
- orders blockade on Southern ports
- assassinated by John Wilkes Booth
- delivers Gettysburg Address
- takes oath for second term as president
- issues the Emancipation Proclamation

November 4, 1842 _____

December 6, 1847 _____

March 4, 1861 _____

April 12, 1861   Civil War begins with the attack on Fort Sumter

April 27, 1861 _____

January 1, 1863 _____

November 19, 1863 _____

March 4, 1865 _____

April 9, 1865   Civil War ends when Robert E. Lee surrenders to Ulysses S. Grant at Appomattox

April 14, 1865 _____

Emancipation and Reconstruction

CODED QUOTES

Lincoln was a great leader and orator. Match each number to its letter to decode some of Lincoln's famous words.

A	B	C	D	E	F	G	H	I	J	K	L	M	N	O	P	Q	R	S	T	U	V	W	X	Y	Z
1	2	3	4	5	6	7	8	9	10	11	12	13	14	15	16	17	18	19	20	21	22	23	24	25	26

1. "1   8-15-21-19-5   4-9-22-9-4-5-4   1-7-1-9-14-19-20   9-20-19-5-12-6

    3-1-14-14-15-20   19-20-1-14-4."

2. "6-1-9-18   16-12-1-25   9-19   1   10-5-23-5-12."

3. "23-15-18-11   23-15-18-11   23-15-18-11   9-19   20-8-5

    13-1-9-14   20-8-9-14-7."

4. "6-15-21-18   19-3-15-18-5   1-14-4   19-5-22-5-14

    25-5-1-18-19   1-7-15...."

Emancipation and Reconstruction

CIVIL WAR EPITAPHS

Here are sayings, or epitaphs, that might have appeared on the tombstones of people who died during the Civil War. Read the epitaph and fill in the name of the person it describes. Research to find the year each person died, and add it to the epitaph.

1. Here lies _____, commander of the great Confederate Army. (1807 – _____)

2. Here lies _____, author of the antislavery novel *Uncle Tom's Cabin*. (1811 – _____)

3. Here lies _____, the Great Emancipator and 16th president of the United States. (1809 – _____)

4. Here lies _____, the Reconstruction president. (1808 – _____)

5. Here lies _____, actor and assassin. (1838 – _____)

6. Here lies _____, president of the Confederate States of America. (1808 – _____)

7. Here lies _____, the mighty general who led the Union to victory at Antietam. (1826 – _____)

8. Here lies _____, "Lady with the Lamp" and battleground angel. (1820 – _____)

9. Here lies _____, the first president of the American Red Cross. (1821 – _____)

10. Here lies _____, commander of the victorious Union army. (1822 – _____)

© Teacher Created Materials, Inc.   35   #2639 U. S. History Brain Teasers

Emancipation and Reconstruction

FREE AND SLAVE STATES

The Northwest Ordinance (1787) made slavery illegal in territories north of the Ohio River. For thirty years, new states were added to the Union as either free states (where slavery was illegal) or slave states (where slavery was legal). Write the name of each state by its shape. Then list each state under the correct heading in the chart to show whether it was a free state or a slave state at the beginning of the Civil War.

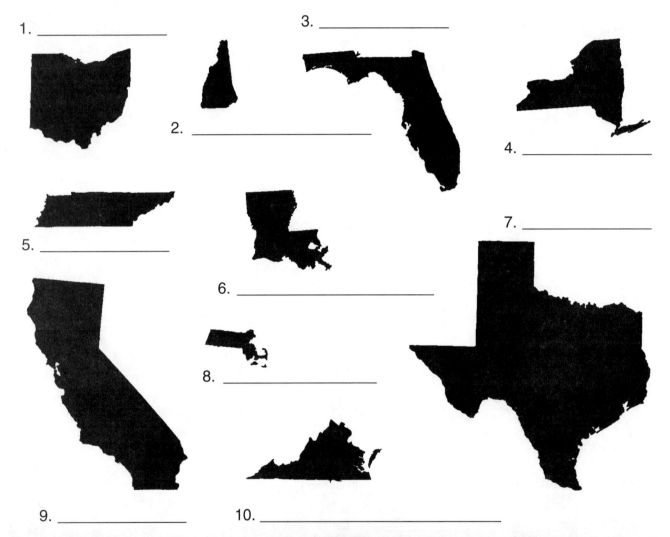

1. _____
2. _____
3. _____
4. _____
5. _____
6. _____
7. _____
8. _____
9. _____
10. _____

Free States	Slave States
1. _____	1. _____
2. _____	2. _____
3. _____	3. _____
4. _____	4. _____
5. _____	5. _____

#2639 U. S. History Brain Teasers © Teacher Created Materials, Inc.

Emancipation and Reconstruction

SPEAKING OF SLAVERY

The issue of slavery divided the country. Look carefully at the letters. Each one contains the answer to the clue, but you will have to find it by reading horizontally, vertically, from the left, or from the right. There may be letters you do not use. Write the answers on the lines.

1. F R E D E R I C K D O U G L A S S R K O a famous black abolitionist	2. A I N B T I O I S L O T a person who wanted to end slavery	3. N C N O I A I P M T A E the act of freeing people from slavery
4. O J O S U R N E U R T R T H C K a reformer who worked to gain rights for slaves and women	5. A B R A H A M L I N C O L N T D the Great Emancipator	6. B X H A R R I E T T U B M A N Q a female conductor on the Underground Railroad
7. D D O S R S T S E C T R slave who took his case to the Supreme Court	8. J O H N B R O W N led an antislavery massacre in Kansas	9. U G D R N R R O D O A A E U I D R N L U secret escape routes for slaves

© Teacher Created Materials, Inc.   37   #2639 U.S. History Brain Teasers

Emancipation and Reconstruction

FROM C TO C

Many changes went into effect following the war between the states. National leaders hoped to rebuild the country and create a positive environment for all people. Write a word for each clue.

1. naturalized resident c __ __ __ ◯ __
2. small log house c __ __ __ ◯
3. northerners who moved south to profit from the war
   c __ __ __ __ ◯ __ __ __ __ __ __
4. place of worship c __ __ __ ◯ __
5. southern states C __ ◯ __ __ __ __ __ __ __ __
6. U.S. lawmakers C __ __ __ ◯ __ __ __
7. school group c __ __ ◯ __
8. illegal act c ◯ __ __ __
9. group of people living together c __ __ __ ◯ __ __ __ __
10. plant grown for food c __ ◯ __
11. young person ⓒ __ __ __ __
12. war between the states C ◯ __ __ __ __ __ __
13. place where people are buried c __ __ ◯ __ __ __
14. a center of justice c ◯ __ __ __

Rearrange the circled letters to answer the following question.
What was the period after the Civil War called?

__ __ __ __ __ __ __ __ __ __ __ __ __ __

Emancipation and Reconstruction

INVENTIVE ANALOGIES

Large cities grew and factories were built at the end of the Civil War. There were plenty of jobs. Several modern inventions played an important part in America's entrance into the modern age. Analogies are comparisons. Use a reference book or an appropriate Web site to help you complete each analogy below.

Example: Washington is to president as George III is to king.

1. _____ is to telephone as Guglielmo Marconi is to radio.

2. Henry Ford is to _____ as George Eastman is to cameras.

3. Cyrus McCormick is to the reaper as Eli Whitney is to the _____.

4. Light bulb and phonograph are to _____ as bifocals and lightning rod are to Benjamin Franklin.

5. _____ is to steam engine as Orville and Wilbur Wright are to airplane.

6. Elias Howe is to sewing machine as _____ is to telegraph.

7. Abner Doubleday is to baseball as Levi Strauss is to _____.

8. Reaper is to crops as _____ is to seeds.

9. Baseball is to _____ as blue jeans are to clothing.

10. _____ is to photograph as Howe is to garment.

11. _____ is to telegram as Bell is to phone call.

12. Telephone is to ear as bifocal is to _____.

© Teacher Created Materials, Inc. 39 #2639 U. S. History Brain Teasers

Emancipation and Reconstruction

ALEXANDER GRAHAM BELL

On March 7, 1876, the United States Patent Office granted Alexander Graham Bell a patent for the telephone, a device that uses electricity to transmit sound. Bell invented the telephone with the help of Thomas Watson, a young mechanic. Use the letters that correspond to the numbers on a real telephone to decode these imaginary telephone numbers. The state where each city is located is in parentheses.

1. 639-9675 _____ (New York)

2. 244-2246 _____ (Illinois)

3. 468-7866 _____ (Texas)

4. 522-5766 _____ (Mississippi)

5. 746-3649 _____ (Arizona)

6. 338-7648 _____ (Michigan)

7. 667-3655 _____ (Virginia)

8. 873-6866 _____ (New Jersey)

9. 285-2682 _____ (Georgia)

10. 636-7447 _____ (Tennessee)

11. 732-8853 _____ (Washington)

12. 726-8233 _____ (New Mexico)

#2639 U. S. History Brain Teasers · · · · · © Teacher Created Materials, Inc.

Emancipation and Reconstruction

THOMAS EDISON

Thomas Alva Edison is one of America's most famous inventors. His work created or improved electric lighting, motion picture projectors, telephones, and phonographs. Most of his inventions are still in use today. Use the letters in Edison's name to help you find the answers to the following questions.

1. What did Edison have 1,033 of? __ __ T __ __ __ __

2. Who was the president of the United States when Edison died? H __ __ __ __ __

3. What is a place where scientists work? __ __ __ O __ __ __ __ __ __

4. What is the name of the city in Ohio where Edison was born? M __ __ __ __

5. What is the first name of Edison's first wife? __ A __ __   Stilwell

6. What did Edison use to help him invent things? S __ __ __ __ __ __

7. Where was Edison's laboratory in New Jersey? __ E __ __ __   Park

8. What is a kind of electric light? __ __ __ __ __ D __ __ __ __ __ __

9. What was the first type of motion picture called? __ I __ __ __ __ __ __ __ __ __ __

10. What was the first name of Edison's father? S __ __ __ __ __

11. Which city had the first electric power system? __ __ __   __ O __ __

12. What is another name for record player? __ __ __ N __ __ __ __ __

© Teacher Created Materials, Inc.   41   #2639 U. S. History Brain Teasers

Emancipation and Reconstruction

STATUE OF LIBERTY

The Statue of Liberty stands on Bedloe's Island in New York Harbor as a symbol of freedom and friendship. In 1886 the statue was given to the people of the United States as a symbol of friendship. Answer the following questions.

1. Where is the island that holds the statue?

   (N)__ __ __ __ __ __ __

2. What does Lady Liberty hold in her left hand?

   __ __ __ __ (e) __

3. What is in the Statue of Liberty's right hand?

   __ __ __ (c) __

4. What are people called who enter another country to live?

   __ __ __ __ __ __ (r)(a) __ __ __

5. What is another word for *liberty*?

   (f) __ __ __ __ __ __ __

Bonus: What country gave the Statue of Liberty to the United States? Rearrange the circled letters to find the answer.

__ __ __ __ __ __

Rearrange the letters in the following words to find the last name of the sculptor who created the Statue of Liberty.

OLD HIT BAR

Frederic-Auguste __ __ __ __ __ __ __ __ __

World Conflict in a New Century

THE ROARING TWENTIES

After World War I, America roared into a period of political and economic activity in which both new technology and new laws made life better for many citizens. Circle the year in which each of the following events occurred.

1. Charles Lindbergh made the first nonstop flight across the Atlantic Ocean.	1926	1927	1929
2. African-American poet Langston Hughes published his first book *The Weary Blues*.	1926	1927	1929
3. The stock market crashed.	1926	1927	1929
4. Bessie Coleman became the first licensed female African-American aviator.	1920	1922	1927
5. The 19th Amendment gave women the right to vote.	1920	1922	1927
6. Babe Ruth hit 60 home runs in a single season for the New York Yankees.	1920	1922	1927
7. Production stopped on the Model-T Ford.	1920	1922	1927
8. Warren G. Harding became president of the United States.	1921	1923	1924
9. Calvin Coolidge became president when Harding died.	1921	1923	1924
10. Congress granted citizenship to Native Americans.	1921	1923	1924
11. The National Origins Act limited the number of immigrants allowed into the United States.	1923	1924	1929
12. Congress authorized Mount Rushmore as a national memorial.	1923	1924	1929

World Conflict in a New Century

MEN OF ACHIEVEMENT

Great wealth or great talent helped many people reach a high level of personal achievement. Circle the name of the man most associated with the businesses, titles, concepts, or places listed.

1. **U.S. Steel**
   Henry Ford   Andrew Carnegie   J.P. Morgan

2. **Ford Motor Company**
   John D. Rockefeller   George Pullman   Henry Ford

3. **Standard Oil Company**
   John D. Rockefeller   Andrew Carnegie   Joseph Pulitzer

4. **Wall Street**
   Andrew Carnegie   J.P. Morgan   Montgomery Ward

5. **Guggenheim Museum**
   Henry Ford   Frank Lloyd Wright   Samuel Gompers

6. **Railroad**
   Cornelius Vanderbilt   Henry Ford   Thomas Edison

7. **Railroad Sleeping Cars**
   Samuel Gompers   George Pullman   Cyrus McCormick

8. **Catalog Sales**
   Andrew Carnegie   Montgomery Ward   Upton Sinclair

9. **American Federation of Labor**
   Samuel Gompers   John D. Rockefeller   Joseph Pulitzer

10. **New York World**
    Frederick Law Olmstead   Joseph Pulitzer   Samuel Gompers

11. ***The Jungle***
    Upton Sinclair   Jack London   John Steinbeck

12. **Central Park**
    Frederick Law Olmstead   George Pullman   Thomas Edison

13. ***The Grapes of Wrath***
    Upton Sinclair   Jack London   John Steinbeck

14. ***Gone with the Wind***
    Clark Gable   Joseph Pulitzer   Henry Ford

15. **Organized Crime**
    John Doe   Al Capone   Cornelius Vanderbilt

#2639 U. S. History Brain Teasers

World Conflict in a New Century

THE DUST BOWL

The Dust Bowl of the 1930s affected life on the plains for nearly ten years. Poor agricultural practices and years of drought caused the land to dry up and blow away. Crops could not grow, and farming people could not make a living.

A. Fill in the blanks with the names of the Dust Bowl states.

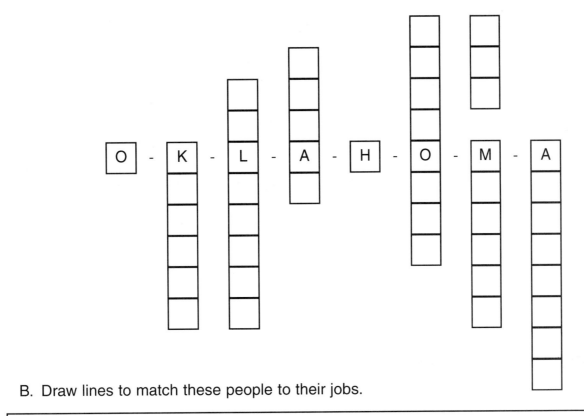

B. Draw lines to match these people to their jobs.

1. Woody Guthrie		novelist who wrote *The Grapes of Wrath*
2. Dorothea Lange		U.S. president
3. John Steinbeck		singer and songwriter
4. Herbert Hoover		journalist who coined the phrase "Dust Bowl"
5. Robert Geiger		documentary photographer

C. Fill in the boxes marked with * to find the people who were most affected by the dust storms.

© Teacher Created Materials, Inc.   #2639 U. S. History Brain Teasers

World Conflict in a New Century

THE GREAT DEPRESSION

In 1929 the stock market crashed. People who owned stock lost their fortunes. Scared people took so much of their money out of banks that soon the banks ran out of money. The country sank into a major economic depression. The Great Depression was a time of great despair. Many people lost their jobs. Without an income, many people went hungry.

Fill in the blanks with words from the clues below. The first clue has something to do with the Great Depression. Change one or two letters in the first answer to make the second word.

1. liquid nourishment __ __ __ __
   cleaning product __ __ __ __ __

2. outerwear __ __ __ __
   heating fuel __ __ __ __

3. unable to find __ __ __ __
   price of goods __ __ __ __

4. economic plan, the New __ __ __ __
   daily food __ __ __ __

5. scrap of bread __ __ __ __ __
   particles of dirt __ __ __ __ __

6. farm product __ __ __ __
   to fall down __ __ __ __

7. monthly payment to landlord __ __ __ __
   temporary shelter made of cloth __ __ __ __ __

8. to conserve __ __ __ __
   to offer at a reduced price __ __ __ __

9. overused __ __ __ __
   toil __ __ __ __

10. small city __ __ __ __
    ripped __ __ __ __

11. wealthy __ __ __ __
    cereal grain __ __ __ __

12. place that holds people's money __ __ __ __
    a bed for one person __ __ __ __

World Conflict in a New Century

WHAT HAPPENED?

At the end of World War I, leaders from around the world gathered to formalize peace by signing a treaty and to consider possible ways to rebuild Europe.

I. Answer the questions below to tell what happened.

Who? _____

_____

What? _____

_____

When? _____

_____

Where? _____

_____

Why? _____

_____

_____

_____

II. What important events occurred on these dates?

1. June 28, 1914	
2. May 7, 1915	
3. April 6, 1917	
4. January 8, 1918	
5. May 31, 1921	

World Conflict in a New Century

WORLD WAR II

On December 7, 1941, Japan attacked Pearl Harbor, an important U.S. naval base in Hawaii. This surprise assault on American territory and people made the United States jump into the four-year conflict that was called World War II. Fill in the blanks to make words. The letters you add will spell words that relate to World War II and match the clue given. The first one has been done for you.

1. German leader A S **H** H **I** S I **T** OW **L** B E **E** E A **R**	2. country that attacked the United States __ O B __ P E __ E N __ S K __ O T	3. weapon of mass destruction R U __ Z O __ H A __ R I __
4. organized group of soldiers __ R M __ U N __ A N __ O U	5. the group of 26 countries which included the United States, that fought together B __ L L S __ I P C __ A W D __ M E B __ A N U __ E D	6. the group of countries, which included Germany, Japan, and Italy, that fought together H __ T A __ E S __ T A __ H
7. the continent adjoining Asia M __ A T H __ R T T __ A P R __ P E S __ O T K __ E P	8. another word for foe __ A R __ O W __ Y E __ A P __ E S	9. to forcibly take over another country __ N K __ U T __ A T __ R T __ I P __ A T
10. groups of soldiers L A __ E T U __ N W O __ L R O __ M C U __ S L I __ T	11. another word for boat A __ K S __ E H __ M A __ E	12. an armored combat vehicle S H I R __ P A S T __ T R A I __ T H A N __

#2639 U. S. History Brain Teasers — 48 — © Teacher Created Materials, Inc.

World Conflict in a New Century

PEOPLE, PLACES, AND THINGS OF WORLD WAR II

The people, places, and things in these lists were important to the United States war effort. Read the lists and add one more item to each.

1. World leaders

    Franklin D. Roosevelt, Winston Churchill, _____

2. Axis countries

    Germany, Japan, _____

3. Rationed products

    sugar, coffee, _____

4. Generals

    George Patton, Douglas MacArthur, _____

5. Battles

    Normandy, Midway, _____

6. Home Front

    victory garden, selective service, _____

7. Aircraft

    B-17, B-29, _____

8. Holocaust

    concentration camps, prisoners, _____

9. G.I. Wear

    helmet, mess kit, _____

10. Manhattan Project

    Enola Gay, Fat Man, _____

11. United Service Organizations

    music, movies, _____

12. Air raid shelter

    food, water, _____

World Conflict in a New Century

WORLD WAR II DATE BOOK

What significant event of World War II happened on each of the following dates?

1.	December 7, 1941	
2.	January 1, 1945	
3.	January 20, 1945	
4.	February 19, 1945	
5.	April 12, 1945	
6.	April 30, 1945	
7.	May 8, 1945	
8.	June 6, 1944	
9.	July 26, 1945	
10.	August 6, 1945	
11.	August 9, 1945	
12.	September 2, 1945	

World Conflict in a New Century

NEW DEAL PROGRAMS

When Franklin Delano Roosevelt became the 32nd president of the United States, America was in the worst economic crisis of its history. Roosevelt and his advisors planned a program to resolve the effects of the Great Depression, reinvigorate the economy, and restore Americans' confidence in their banks.

I. Follow these steps.

1. Draw a line through seven groups of initials that represent programs in a plan to help the country out of economic depression.
2. Draw a line through the initials of the president who developed the plan.
3. Circle the letter between each set of initials.

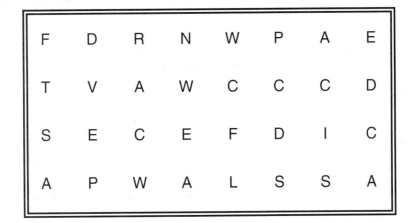

4. Print the circled letters on the lines below to find the name of Roosevelt's recovery plan for America.

The __ __ __   __ __ __ __

II. Now answer these questions.

1. Which program provided flood control on the Tennessee River? _____
2. Which program insured bank deposits? _____
3. Which program established old-age pensions? _____
4. Which program supported actors, writers, musicians, and artists? _____
5. Which program improved America's parklands? _____
6. Which program gave a job to every able-bodied man not working in private industry? _____
7. Which program protected investors? _____

Establishment of a Modern Society

A IS FOR ALASKA

In 1867 William Seward purchased Alaska for the United States, but the territory did not become a state until January 3, 1959. Complete this story about our 49th state by filling in words that begin with the letter **A** from the word bank.

A __ a __ __ a is in North A __ __ __ __ __ a. It is our 49th and largest state, having a land a __ __ a of 365,000,000 a __ __ __ __. The largest city by population is A __ __ __ __ __ a __ __. President A __ __ __ __ __ Jackson bought the land from Russian Czar A __ __ __ a __ __ __ __ II in 1867. Part of the coast is on the A __ __ __ __ __ Ocean.

Two groups of native people are the A __ __ __ __ and the A __ __ a __ a __ __ a __. Their a __ __ __ __ __ __ __ came from A __ __ a. There are 1800 named islands, including A __ __ __ and A __ a __ __ __ __ a __. In the fall, winter, and spring, the A __ __ __ __ a Borealis, or the Northern Lights, can be seen in the night sky.

Word Bank

Alexander	America	Aurora
Alaska	Athabascan	ancestors
Amatignak	acres	Aleut
Andrew	Anchorage	area
Arctic	Attu	Asia

Bonus: Find three other states whose names or nicknames begin and end with the letter **A**.

• A __ __ __ __ __ a is a southwestern state.

• A __ __ __ __ __ a is a southern state.

• "A __ __ __ a State" is the nickname for our only state that is a chain of islands.

#2639 U. S. History Brain Teasers 52 © Teacher Created Materials, Inc.

Establishment of a Modern Society

THE ALOHA STATE

Hawaii is a group of islands in the Pacific Ocean southwest of the United States mainland. Hawaii became our 50th state on August 21, 1959.

I. Use a map to label the eight islands.

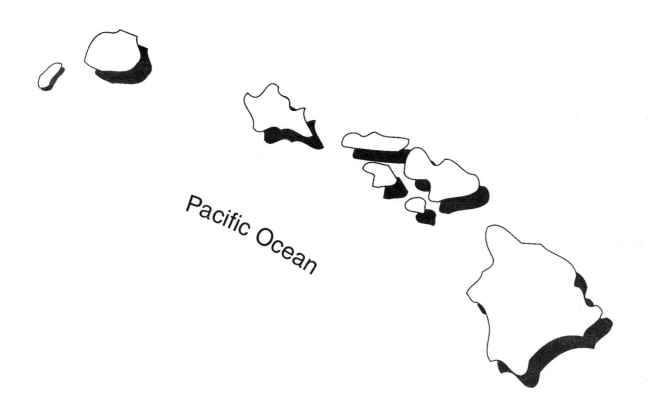

II. Do research to find the nicknames of the six islands listed below. Draw a line to match each island to its nickname.

Kauai	The Big Island
Oahu	The Capital Island
Molokai	The Friendly Island
Maui	The Garden Island
Lanai	The Pineapple Island
Hawaii	The Valley Island

© Teacher Created Materials, Inc. 53 #2639 U. S. History Brain Teasers

Establishment of a Modern Society

THEY HAVE OVERCOME

Circle the word that best describes these leaders of the Civil Rights Movement.

1. Dr. Martin Luther King, Jr.		
lawyer	minister	industrialist
2. Thurgood Marshall		
president	senator	Supreme Court judge
3. Linda Brown		
student	athlete	dancer
4. Marian Wright Edelman		
child advocate	legal secretary	television star
5. Adam Clayton Powell, Jr.		
congressman	president	CEO of General Motors
6. Alex Haley		
doctor	lawyer	author
7. Nikki Giovanni		
singer	poet	television star
8. Wilma Rudolph		
athlete	cashier	dancer
9. Sidney Poitier		
minister	actor	author
10. Shirley Chisholm		
actress	congresswoman	musician
11. Rosa Parks		
seamstress	store clerk	cook
12. Julian Bond		
senator	athlete	rock musician

Establishment of a Modern Society

EQUAL IS RIGHT

Civil rights became a major political issue in the 1960s. African-American leaders organized marches, sit-ins, and freedom rides to promote their quest for equality and justice.

I. Answer the clues. Count the number of letters you wrote on each line and write that number after the equals sign. Add the numbers for items 1 – 4 to get the total.

1. She refused to give her bus seat to a white man.   Rosa _____ = ____

2. He preached and practiced nonviolence.   M.L._____, Jr. = ____

3. This is an abbreviation for the country's oldest civil rights group.   _____ = ____

4. This is where most civil rights protests occurred.   _____ = ____

   Total = ____

II. Write the name of the struggle for civil rights in the 1960s on the lines. Count the number of letters in the name. The number should equal the total from above.

_____ _____ _____ = ____

III. Here is a summary of the Civil Rights Act. The law's purpose is to ban discrimination based on the grounds of race, color, or national origin in programs or activities receiving federal financial assistance.

In what year did the Civil Rights Act become law? _____

Establishment of a Modern Society

A PERFECT SCORE

Use facts about our government to complete this puzzle. Add or subtract the numbers to get a perfect score.

_____ amendments in the Bill of Rights

+ _____ states in the United States

+ _____ presidential terms allowed by the Constitution

+ _____ white stripes on the U.S. flag

+ _____ original colonies

+ _____ letters in the alphabet

+ _____ countries bordering the United States

+ _____ branches of government

+ _____ one dozen

= 100   A Perfect Score!

Establishment of a Modern Society

THE REAGAN YEARS

Ronald Wilson Reagan was elected 40th president of the United States in 1980. He was an extremely popular president who was elected to a second term.

I. Circle the words that give facts about the life of President Reagan.

1. The name of the First Lady

    Judy *Nancy* *Mary*

2. Reagan was governor of this state

    California *Massachusetts* *Illinois*

3. Reagan's nickname

    Dude *Dutch* *Goldie*

4. Reagan's political party

    Democrat *Republican* *Libertarian*

5. Reagan's vice-president

    John Adams *Bob Dole* *George Bush*

6. Reagan's career before politics

    writer *lawyer* *actor*

7. Reagan's opponent in 1984

    Barry Goldwater *Oliver North* *Walter Mondale*

II. Give the date for each of these newspaper headlines about Reagan's presidency.

1. Assassination Attempt on President Reagan _____

2. World Cheers as Berlin Wall Tumbles _____

3. Reagan Names First Woman to Supreme Court _____

4. Challenger Spacecraft Explodes _____

5. Inauguration Brings Iranian Hostage Release _____

6. Carter Defeated in Landslide Vote _____

Establishment of a Modern Society

FAMOUS WOMEN

Choose answers from **Box A** and **Box B** to complete the chart with the last names and the contributions of these famous American women.

	Last Name	Contribution
1. Jane		
2. Susan B.		
3. Clara		
4. Nellie		
5. Pearl		
6. Annie		
7. Mary		
8. Emily		
9. Eleanor		
10. Margaret		
11. Amelia		
12. Bessie		
13. Mother		
14. Louisa May		
15. Madame C.J.		

Box A	
Barton	Smith
Alcott	Earhart
Anthony	Jones
Addams	Walker
Cassatt	Oakley
Roosevelt	Buck
Dickinson	Bly
Sanger	

Box B	
First Lady	social reformer
painter	suffragette
poet	nurse
social activist	author
singer	aviator
novelist	entrepreneur
sharpshooter	humanitarian
journalist	

#2639 U. S. History Brain Teasers   58   © Teacher Created Materials, Inc.

Establishment of a Modern Society

FIRST LADIES' FIRST NAMES

Write the first names of the First Ladies on the lines.

1. George and _____ Washington
2. John and _____ Adams
3. James and _____ Madison
4. James and _____ Polk
5. Millard and _____ Fillmore
6. Abraham and _____ Lincoln
7. Ulysses and _____ Grant
8. Warren G. and _____ Harding
9. Calvin and _____ Coolidge
10. E _____ Roosevelt
11. E _____ Truman
12. M _____ Eisenhower
13. J _____ Kennedy
14. C _____ Johnson
15. T _____ Nixon
16. E _____ Ford
17. R _____ Carter
18. N _____ Reagan
19. B _____ Bush
20. H _____ Clinton

Bonus: What were the nicknames of these First Ladies?

_____ Johnson   _____ Nixon

Establishment of a Modern Society

ASSASSINATED PRESIDENTS

The vice-president takes office whenever the president of the United States is unable to perform his duties. Four U.S. presidents have been assassinated. On the lines under each group, write what the names, dates, or places have in common.

1. Abraham Lincoln, James Garfield, William McKinley, John Kennedy

   _____
   _____

2. April 14, 1865; July 2, 1881; September 6, 1901; November 22, 1963

   _____
   _____

3. Andrew Johnson, Chester Arthur, Theodore Roosevelt, Lyndon Johnson

   _____
   _____

4. John Wilkes Booth, Charles Guiteau, Leon Czolgosz, Lee Harvey Oswald

   _____
   _____

5. Washington, D.C.; Washington, D.C.; Buffalo, New York; Dallas, Texas

   _____
   _____

6. Ford's Theater, railroad station, Temple of Music, motorcade

   _____
   _____

7. Kentucky, Ohio, Ohio, Massachusetts

   _____
   _____

8. Mary, Lucretia, Ida, Jacqueline

   _____
   _____

Establishment of a Modern Society

CATEGORIES

Fill each blank with the name of a United States president.

I. Each pair of these presidents has the same last name.

1. _____ and _____
2. _____ and _____
3. _____ and _____
4. _____ and _____

II. These presidents have only four letters in their last names.

5. _____
6. _____
7. _____
8. _____

III. These presidents have last names that begin with a vowel.

9. _____
10. _____
11. _____
12. _____

IV. These presidents each have a first and last name that begin with the same letter.

13. _____
14. _____
15. _____
16. _____

Challenge Questions:

Which president has a last name with four syllables? _____

Which president was elected to four terms? _____

Establishment of a Modern Society

PICTURE PUZZLE

Cut out the puzzle pieces. Glue them together on a piece of construction paper. Write the name of this important landmark in Washington, D.C., on the construction paper. Also write five facts about this building.

Establishment of a Modern Society

CHAIN OF STATE NAMES

Use the last letter of the first word in the chain to begin the next word. Complete the chain with names of states. The first one has been done for you.

1. U T A H

2. H __ __ __ __ I

3. I __ __ __ O

4. O __ __ O

5. O __ __ __ __ N

6. N __ __ __ __ __ K

7. K __ __ __ __ S

8. S __ __ __ __ __ __ __ __ __ A

9. A __ __ __ A

10. A __ __ __ __ A

11. A __ __ __ __ __ __ S

12. S __ __ __ __ __ __ __ __ A

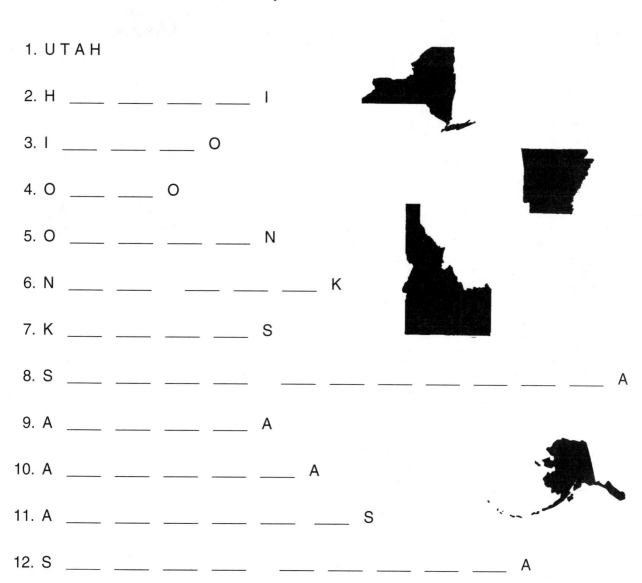

Challenge Activity: Begin a new chain with the name of your state. Add as many more state names as you can.

© Teacher Created Materials, Inc.   63   #2639 U. S. History Brain Teasers

Establishment of a Modern Society

NUMBERS OF LETTERS

First read all the directions so you do not put the name of a state in the wrong place. Then write the name of a state in the blank where it belongs best.

I. These state names have double letters.

1. _____
2. _____
3. _____
4. _____
5. _____
6. _____

II. This state has two sets of double letters.

7. _____

III. These states have three sets of double letters.

8. _____
9. _____

IV. Many state names have only four vowels. How many can you name?

_____   _____
_____   _____
_____   _____
_____   _____
_____   _____
_____   _____
_____   _____

#2639 U. S. History Brain Teasers   64   © Teacher Created Materials, Inc.

Establishment of a Modern Society

PRESIDENTIAL HOPEFULS

I. Fill in the blanks to tell about the unsuccessful presidential candidate from the 1992 election.

1. He was a b __ __ __ __ __ __ __ __ __ __ from Texas.
                                         1

2. He wanted to keep j __ __ __ in America.
                             2   3

3. He wanted to cut f __ __ __ __ __ __ spending.
                             4

4. He was the third- __ __ __ __ y candidate.
                     5   6

Answer: __ __ __ __ __ __ __ __ __
                  1 2 3 3 5 4 1 2 6

II. Fill in the blanks to tell about the unsuccessful presidential candidate from the 1996 election.

1. He was a R __ __ __ __ __ __ __ __ __ senator in the U.S. Congress.
                           1   2

2. He wanted to balance the n __ __ __ __ __ __ __ budget.
                                   3   4

3. His wife was called L __ __ __ __ , which is a nickname for Elizabeth.
                         5

Answer: __ __ __ __ __ __ __
                  2 3 2 5 3 4 1

General Knowledge

WAR DATES

On the blanks, write the year that each of these wars began. Then add or subtract the numbers as indicated to find the year World War II ended.

    _____   Civil War

+ _____   The War of 1812

− _____   The American Revolution

+ _____   World War II

− _____   World War I

+ _____   Persian Gulf War

− _____   Vietnam War

−   3

= _____   Year of VJ Day, or Victory over Japan Day, when the Japanese surrendered

---

Use a reference book to help you fill in the date for each of these World War II headlines.

1. _____   FDR Declares War on Japan—Pearl Harbor Bombed

2. _____   U.S. Troops Land on Iwo Jima

3. _____   Allies Invade Western Europe on D-Day

4. _____   Soviet Forces Free Jews at Auschwitz

5. _____   U.S. Drops A-Bomb—Japan Surrenders

General Knowledge

FAMOUS AMERICAN FIRSTS

Complete each statement by answering who, what, when, or where.

I. Who? (Tell the person's name.)

1. The first woman to fly solo across the Atlantic Ocean

2. The first woman appointed Supreme Court justice

3. The first American woman in space

4. The first vice president of the United States

5. The first person to walk on the moon

II. What?

6. Pilgrims first celebrated this holiday in Plymouth, Massachusetts in 1621.

7. Charles Goodyear first vulcanized this product in 1839.

8. Elias Howe invented the first of these machines in 1845.

9. Alexander Graham Bell first demonstrated this invention in 1876.

10. Dr. Vannevar Bush first developed the "non-electronic differential analyzer" in 1928.

General Knowledge

FAMOUS AMERICAN FIRSTS *(cont.)*

III. When? (Tell the year.)

11. Virginia Dare was the first person born in America to English parents.

12. Charles Lindbergh made the first nonstop transatlantic flight.

13. John Glenn flew the first manned orbital mission in *Friendship 7*.

14. South Carolina became the first state to secede from the Union.

15. The first Pizza Hut opened in Wichita, Kansas.

IV. Where? (Tell the location.)

16. The first free public school founded

17. The first state to join the Union

18. The first national park

19. The first metal-framed skyscraper

20. The first McDonald's restaurant

General Knowledge

THIS LAND IS YOUR LAND

Find 16 mistakes in this map of the United States.

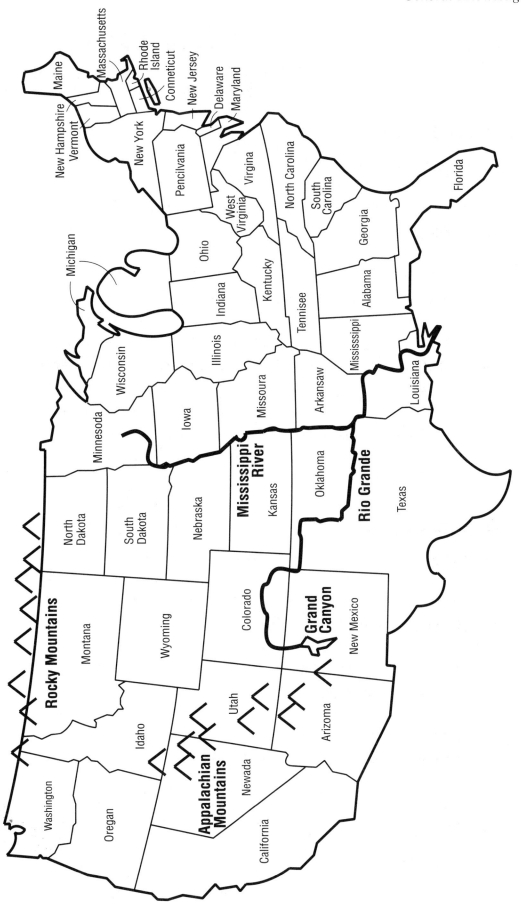

© Teacher Created Materials, Inc. 69 #2639 U. S. History Brain Teasers

General Knowledge

PLACES OF HISTORIC IMPORTANCE

Memorials, monuments, and landmarks are a part of America's history. Use the clues to help you add a title and location for each list.

1. Title: _____
   Location: _____
   - Monticello
   - cherry trees
   - Declaration of Independence

2. Title: _____
   Location: _____
   - Civil War
   - Gettysburg Address
   - Assassinated president

3. Title: _____
   Location: _____
   - Black Hills
   - four faces
   - Gutzon Borglum

4. Title: _____
   Location: _____
   - tablet
   - torch
   - Ellis Island

5. Title: _____
   Location: _____
   - African-American scientist
   - sweet potatoes
   - peanuts

6. Title: _____
   Location: _____
   - marble
   - obelisk
   - birthday dedication

7. Title: _____
   Location: _____
   - 1600 Pennsylvania Avenue
   - rose garden
   - oval office

8. Title: _____
   Location: _____
   - nonviolent leader
   - Baptist minister
   - civil rights protests

9. Title: _____
   Location: _____
   - unnamed grave
   - guarded tomb
   - Arlington National Cemetery

10. Title: _____
    Location: _____
    - light bulb
    - telephone
    - motion picture projector

General Knowledge

LICENSE PLATE DECODER

A car license plate tells something about its owner. Decode the clues on the imaginary license plates.
Bonus: Name a person to whom each imaginary plate could belong.

1. _____   2. _____   3. _____

_____   _____   _____

4. _____   5. _____   6. _____

_____   _____   _____

7. _____   8. _____   9. _____

_____   _____   _____

10. _____   11. _____   12. _____

_____   _____   _____

© Teacher Created Materials, Inc.   71   #2639 U. S. History Brain Teasers

General Knowledge

NATIONAL SYMBOLS

A symbol is something that stands for or represents something else. Read the clues and name these national symbols.

1. red for courage, white for liberty, blue for justice _____

2. Philadelphia, cracked copper, rings _____

3. Republican Party, mascot, animal _____

4. Democratic Party, mascot, animal _____

5. olive branch, arrows, bald eagle _____

6. thunderbird, white head, big wings _____

7. Sam Wilson, army, striped costume _____

8. meat, hide, wild animal _____

9. Pilgrims, ship, Plymouth Rock _____

10. immigrants, French, lady with a lamp _____

#2639 U. S. History Brain Teasers   72   © *Teacher Created Materials, Inc.*

General Knowledge

ANALOGIES

Many men and women have played important parts in American history. Complete these analogies.

Example: Cesar Chavez is to Hispanic as Martin Luther King, Jr. is to African American.

1. Jane Addams is to _____ as Susan B. Anthony is to women.

2. Rosa Parks is to _____ as Cesar Chavez is to labor strike.

3. Martin Luther King, Jr. is to _____ as Betty Friedan is to women's liberation.

4. Thurgood Marshall is to _____ as Jackie Robinson is to Brooklyn Dodgers.

5. Linda Brown is to school desegregation as _____ is to bus boycott.

6. _____ is to American Federation of Labor as John L. Lewis is to United Mine Workers.

7. Theodore Roosevelt is to _____ as John Quincy Adams is to Erie Canal.

8. Roger Williams is to Puritan as _____ is to Baptist.

9. William Lloyd Garrison is to *The Liberator* as _____ is to the Emancipation Proclamation.

10. _____ is to Boston Massacre as Nat Turner is to slave revolt.

11. Thomas Paine is to *Common Sense* as _____ is to *Poor Richard's Almanac*.

12. Roger Williams is to Rhode Island as William Penn is to _____ .

13. Molly Pitcher is to _____ as Rosie O'Neal Greenhow is to Civil War.

14. John Brown is to _____ as Henry Clay is to the Missouri Compromise.

© Teacher Created Materials, Inc.   73   #2639 *U. S. History Brain Teasers*

General Knowledge

TRIVIA

1. "We the People of the United States" are the first seven words to what important document? _____
2. Who was the first American to walk on the moon? _____
3. Name two Americans to appear on U.S. coins who were not presidents. _____
4. What is the only state that borders only one other state? _____
5. How are the fifty stars on the U.S. flag arranged? _____
6. What were the two capital cities before Washington, D.C.? _____
7. How tall is the Washington Memorial? _____
8. Who wrote "The Star-Spangled Banner"? _____
9. In which hand does Miss Liberty hold her torch? _____
10. In what state would Washington, D.C., be found? _____
11. What do we call a government in which the people elect their leaders? _____
12. What famous words appear on the Great Seal of the United States? _____
13. What is the only "island" state that is not an island? _____
14. Who flew the first airplane? _____
15. Who killed President Lincoln? _____

#2639 U. S. History Brain Teasers 74 © Teacher Created Materials, Inc.

General Knowledge

PEOPLE IN PICTURES

Decode these rebus puzzles to find the names of people important in American history.

1. George				_____
2. Jimmy		+ ter		_____
3. Ulysses S. Gr +				_____
4. Harriet		+		_____
5. Davey C +		+ t		_____
6.		+	+ an	_____
7. + er T.		+ ing +		_____
8. Christopher		− n +		_____
9. Charles		+		+ is _____

© Teacher Created Materials, Inc.   75   #2639 U. S. History Brain Teasers

ANSWER KEY

Coming to America (page 3)

welcome—
French: bienvenue
German: willkommen
Spanish: bienvenido

America—
French: Amérique
German: Amerika
Spanish: América

freedom—
French: liberté
German: die Freiheit
Spanish: libertad

immigrant—
French: immigré
German: der Einwanderer
Spanish: immigrante

democracy—
French: democratie
German: die Demokratie
Spanish: democrácia

Geography Word Pairs (page 4)
1. south, mouth
2. lake, lane
3. mile, mule
4. explore, explode
5. map, cap
6. west, best
7. land, hand
8. sea, tea
9. mountain, fountain
10. pole, hole
11. state, slate
12. line, lime

Geography Terms (page 5)

Puzzle: Geographic Terms

Riddle: An island is a body of land surrounded by water, and a lake is a body of water surrounded by land.

History Homophones (page 6)
1. peace
2. seize
3. plain
4. sail
5. world
6. herd
7. site
8. horse
9. strait
10. build
11. fir
12. poor
13. reign
14. tax
15. capitol
16. cede
17. corp
18. route
19. throne
20. war

New World Changes (page 7)
1. truck
2. mister
3. store
4. lend
5. mop
6. loader
7. firm
8. see
9. bottle
10. burn or barn
11. role
12. rain
13. puddle
14. trip
15. shout

Traditional Foods (page 8)
1. Kim's family—China
2. Pietro's family—Russia
3. Sofia's family—Italy
4. Rosita's family—Mexico
5. Sean's family—Ireland
6. Hans's family—Germany

Europeans Explore a New Land (page 9)

Possible answers:
1. car, cart, art, tie, tier
2. no, nor, or, north, we, west, pass, sage, age
3. champ, ham, am, amp, plain, lain, in
4. ran, an, is, or, on, ad, do
5. ran, an, is, rake
6. is, stop, to, top, he, her, bus, us
7. span, pan, an, is, harm, arm, mad, ad
8. scan, can, an, and, in
9. rope, pea, an
10. net, the, he, her, lands, land, an, and

Native American Life (page 10)
1. teepee
2. bow and arrow
3. glass beads
4. land
5. nomads
6. sign language
7. buffalo
8. horse
9. long house
10. mesa
11. salmon
12. moccasin
13. maize
14. potlatch
15. squash

Bonus: treaty

Culture Groups (page 11)
1. Pueblo
2. Arapaho
3. Comanche
4. Cheyenne
5. Pawnee
6. Apache
7. Crow
8. Sioux
9. Osage
10. Creek

Word Clues (page 12)
1. mice
2. rain
3. meat
4. train
5. tan
6. rice
7. time
8. vine
9. name
10. man
11. nice
12. ear
13. arm
14. vein
15. main
16. can
17. tear
18. car
19. neat
20. certain

Picture Memory (page 13)

corn, buffalo, canoe, horse, deer, squash, fish, moccasin, feather, teepee, bow and arrow

Colonial Rhymes (page 14)
1. keep sheep
2. raise maize
3. green bean
4. school tool
5. crop shop
6. fish dish
7. ship trip
8. grand land
9. plains trains
10. church search

Early American Anagrams (page 15)
1. James Madison
2. Nathan Hale
3. Benjamin Franklin
4. Thomas Jefferson
5. George Washington
6. Samuel Adams
7. Paul Revere
8. Alexander Hamilton
9. Thomas Paine
10. John Adams
11. Ethan Allen
12. James Monroe

Thirteen Original Colonies (page 16)

Pennsylvania

Colonial Hidden Meanings (page 17)
1. peninsula
2. Virginia
3. thirteen original colonies
4. sail up river
5. lost in the wilderness
6. seated around a campfire
7. walk between rows of corn
8. Puritans
9. cabin in the woods

Categorize Favorite Things (page 18)

Music/Dance
1. spinet
2. minuet
3. reel
4. jig

ANSWER KEY (cont.)

Categorize Favorite Things (cont.)

Food
1. shepherd's pie
2. trifle
3. porridge
4. cobbler

School
1. hornbook
2. quill
3. cipher
4. primer

Games/Toys
1. stilts
2. quoits
3. checks
4. scotch hopping

Clothing
1. muff
2. breeches
3. tricorne
4. clogs

Pilgrims Rebus (page 19)
1. tobacco
2. shelter
3. firearms
4. harvest
5. spear fishing
6. log cabin
7. candle
8. pumpkin
9. cabbage
10. potatoes

Patrick Henry (page 20)
"Give me liberty, or give me death!"
1. lawyer
2. Virginia
3. Stamp Act
4. freedom
5. orator

Boston Tea Party (page 21)
1. Redcoats
2. Parliament
3. East India Company
4. representation
5. Committees of Correspondence
6. boycott
7. Sons of Liberty
8. Samuel Adams
9. Intolerable Acts
10. income tax
11. sales tax

Constitutionally Correct (page 22)

21 + 22 + 19 – 25 + 24 – 23 + 18 + 20 – 26 = 50

The Star-Spangled Banner (page 23)

see, dawn's, hailed, twilight's, stripes, stars, perilous, ramparts, streaming, rocket's, bombs, proof, flag, star, land, home

1. 1775–1777
2. 1777
3. 1837
4. 1848
5. 1865
6. 1912–1959

The American Revolution (page 24)
1. Washington
2. Lexington
3. Yorktown
4. Independence
5. Minutemen
6. King
7. Redcoats
8. Treaty
9. Paine
10. Revere

Surfin' the Colonies (page 25)
1. New Hampshire
2. Massachusetts
3. New York
4. Rhode Island
5. Connecticut
6. New Jersey
7. Delaware
8. Maryland
9. Virginia
10. North Carolina
11. South Carolina
12. Georgia
13. Pennsylvania

1. Delaware, December 7, 1787
2. Pennsylvania, December 12, 1787
3. New Jersey, December 18, 1787

Split Proverbs (page 26)
1. Have you something to do tomorrow, do it today.
2. A true friend is the best possession.
3. No gain, without pain.
4. Be always ashamed to catch thyself idle.
5. People who are wrapped up in themselves make small packages.
6. A penny saved is a penny earned.
7. Early to bed and early to rise, makes a man healthy, wealthy, and wise.
8. 'Tis easier to prevent bad habits than to break them.
9. An ounce of prevention is worth a pound of cure.
10. A bird in the hand is worth two in the bush.

Read All About It! (page 27)
1. 1848
2. 1836
3. 1825
4. 1804-1806
5. 1789
6. 1788
7. 1801
8. 1814
9. 1781
10. 1787
11. 1812
12. 1814

Quotable Quotes (page 28)
1. Patrick Henry
2. Nathan Hale
3. Abraham Lincoln
4. George Washington
5. Benjamin Franklin
6. Benjamin Franklin
7. Abraham Lincoln
8. Frederick Douglass
9. Sojourner Truth
10. John Adams

Important Treaty (page 29)

Who—Thomas Jefferson, James Monroe, Meriwether Lewis, William Clark, Robert Livingston

What—Louisiana Purchase

When—Dated: April 30, 1803; Signed: May 2, 1803

Where—From the Mississippi River west to the Rocky Mountains

How Much—828,000 square miles for $15 million

Bonus: Arkansas, Iowa, Louisiana, Missouri, Montana, Nebraska, North Dakota, South Dakota, Oklahoma, part of Colorado, Kansas, Minnesota, Wyoming

Mississippi River Geography (page 30)

States: Minnesota, Wisconsin, Iowa, Illinois, Missouri, Kentucky, Tennessee, Arkansas, Louisiana, Mississippi

Cities: Minneapolis, MN; St. Louis, MO; Cairo, IL; Memphis, TN; Natchez, MS; New Orleans, LA;

Women's Rights (page 31)
1. Harriet Beecher Stowe
2. Jane Addams
3. Lucretia Mott and Elizabeth Cady Stanton
4. Sojourner Truth
5. Carry Nation
6. Margaret Sanger
7. Susan B. Anthony
8. Harriet Tubman
9. Jeannette Rankin

Settling the West (page 32)
1. d
2. j
3. h
4. k
5. g
6. e
7. l
8. b
9. i
10. c
11. f
12. a

Abraham Lincoln Time Line (page 33)

11/4/1842 marries Mary Todd

12/6/1847 wins election to House of Representatives

ANSWER KEY (cont.)

Lincoln (cont.)
3/4/1861 becomes 16th U.S. president
4/27/1861 orders blockade on the Southern ports
1/1/1863 issues Emancipation Proclamation
11/19/1863 delivers Gettysburg Address
3/4/1865 takes oath for second term as president
4/14/1865 assassinated by John Wilkes Booth

Coded Quotes (page 34)
1. "A house divided against itself cannot stand."
2. "Fair play is a jewel."
3. "Work, work, work is the main thing."
4. "Four score and seven years ago…."

Civil War Epitaphs (page 35)
1. Robert E. Lee 1870
2. Harriet Beecher Stowe 1896
3. Abraham Lincoln 1865
4. Andrew Johnson 1875
5. John Wilkes Booth 1865
6. Jefferson Davis 1889
7. General George B. McClellan 1885
8. Florence Nightingale 1910
9. Clara Barton 1912
10. Ulysses S. Grant 1885

Free and Slave States (page 36)
1. OH   6. LA
2. NH   7. TX
3. FL   8. MA
4. NY   9. CA
5. TN   10. VA

Free States: California, Ohio, Massachusetts, New York, New Hampshire
Slave States: Texas, Florida, Louisiana, Virginia, Tennessee

Speaking of Slavery (page 37)
1. Frederick Douglass
2. abolitionist
3. emancipation
4. Sojourner Truth
5. Abraham Lincoln
6. Harriet Tubman
7. Dred Scott
8. John Brown
9. Underground Railroad

From C to C (page 38)
1. citizen
2. cabin
3. carpetbaggers
4. church
5. Confederacy
6. Congress
7. class
8. crime
9. community
10. crop
11. child
12. Civil War
13. cemetery
14. court

Reconstruction

Inventive Analogies (page 39)
1. Alexander Graham Bell
2. automobiles
3. cotton gin
4. Thomas Edison
5. Robert Fulton
6. Samuel Morse
7. blue jeans
8. cotton gin
9. game or sports
10. Eastman
11. Morse
12. eye

Alexander Graham Bell (page 40)
1. New York
2. Chicago
3. Houston
4. Jackson
5. Phoenix
6. Detroit
7. Norfolk
8. Trenton
9. Atlanta
10. Memphis
11. Seattle
12. Santa Fe

Thomas Edison (page 41)
1. patents
2. Hoover
3. laboratory
4. Milan
5. Mary
6. science
7. Menlo
8. incandescent
9. kinetiscope
10. Samuel
11. New York
12. phonograph

Statue of Liberty (page 42)
1. New York
2. tablet
3. torch
4. immigrants
5. freedom

Bonus: France
Bartholdi

The Roaring Twenties (page 43)
1. 1927
2. 1926
3. 1929
4. 1922
5. 1920
6. 1927
7. 1927
8. 1921
9. 1923
10. 1924
11. 1924
12. 1929

Men of Achievement (page 44)
1. Andrew Carnegie
2. Henry Ford
3. John D. Rockefeller
4. J.P. Morgan
5. Frank Lloyd Wright
6. Cornelius Vanderbilt
7. George Pullman
8. Montgomery Ward
9. Samuel Gompers
10. Joseph Pulitzer
11. Upton Sinclair
12. Frederick Law Olmstead
13. John Steinbeck
14. Clark Gable
15. Al Capone

The Dust Bowl (page 45)
A. Kansas, Colorado, Texas, Missouri, New Mexico, Arkansas
B. 1. singer and songwriter
   2. documentary photographer
   3. novelist who wrote *The Grapes of Wrath*
   4. U.S. president
   5. journalist who coined the phrase "Dust Bowl"
C. FARMERS

The Great Depression (page 46)
1. soup, soap
2. coat, coal
3. lost, cost
4. Deal, meal
5. crust, dust
6. crop, drop
7. rent, tent
8. save, sale
9. worn, work
10. town, torn
11. rich, rice
12. bank, bunk

What Happened? (page 47)
I. **Who**—Lloyd George, Great Britain; Vittorio Orlando, Italy; Georges Clemenceau, France; Woodrow Wilson, United States
What—Treaty of Versailles was signed
When—June 28, 1919
Where—Paris, France
Why—to end World War I

II. 1. Archduke Ferdinand was assassinated.
2. The Germans sank the *Lusitania*.
3. United States declared war on Germany.
4. President Wilson presents the Fourteen Points to Congress.
5. The Sacco-Vanzetti trial began.

ANSWER KEY (cont.)

World War II (page 48)

1. Hitler
2. Japan
3. bomb
4. army
5. Allies
6. Axis
7. Europe
8. enemy
9. invade
10. troops
11. ship
12. tank

People, Places, and Things of World War II (page 49)

Answers will vary.

World War II Date Book (page 50)

1. Japan attacks Pearl Harbor; United States enters World War II
2. Battle of the Bulge
3. FDR is inaugurated to 4th term as president
4. Americans land on Iwo Jima
5. FDR dies, Harry Truman becomes president
6. Hitler commits suicide in Berlin
7. Victory in Europe (V-E Day)
8. D-Day, Allied troops invade France
9. Peace Conference begins at Potsdam, Germany
10. Enola Gay bombs Hiroshima
11. Nagasaki is bombed
12. V-J Day, Japan surrenders

New Deal Programs (page 51)

I. FDR, WPA, TVA, CCC, SEC, FDIC, PWA, SSA

The New Deal

II. 1. Tennessee Valley Authority (TVA)
2. Federal Deposit Insurance Corporation (FDIC)
3. Social Security Act (SSA)
4. Public Works Administration (PWA)
5. Civilian Conservation Corps (CCC)
6. Works Progress Administration (WPA)
7. Securities and Exchange Commission (SEC)

A Is for Alaska (page 52)

Alaska
America
area
acres
Anchorage
Andrew
Alexander
Arctic
Aleut
Athabascan
ancestors
Asia
Attu
Amatignak
Aurora

Bonus: Arizona, Alabama, Aloha

The Aloha State (page 53)

Kauai—The Garden Island
Oahu—The Capital Island
Molokai—The Friendly Island
Maui—The Valley Island
Lanai—The Pineapple Island
Hawaii—The Big Island

They Have Overcome (page 54)

1. minister
2. Supreme Court judge
3. student
4. child advocate
5. congressman
6. author
7. poet
8. athlete
9. actor
10. congresswoman
11. seamstress
12. senator

Equal is Right (page 55)

I. 1. Parks = 5
2. King = 4
3. NAACP = 5
4. South = 5

Total = 19

II. 1. Civil Rights Movement = 19

III. 1964

A Perfect Score (page 56)

$10 + 50 + 2 + 6 + 13 + 26 + 2 + 3 - 12 = 100$

The Reagan Years (page 57)

I. 1. Nancy
2. California
3. Dutch
4. Republican
5. George Bush
6. actor
7. Walter Mondale

II. 1. March 30, 1981
2. November 9, 1989
3. July 7, 1981
4. January 28, 1986
5. January 20, 1981
6. November 4, 1980

Famous Women (page 58)

1. Jane Addams, social reformer
2. Susan B. Anthony, suffragette
3. Clara Barton, nurse
4. Nellie Bly, journalist
5. Pearl Buck, novelist or author
6. Annie Oakley, sharpshooter
7. Mary Cassatt, painter
8. Emily Dickinson, poet
9. Eleanor Roosevelt, First Lady
10. Margaret Sanger, social activist
11. Amelia Earhart, aviator
12. Bessie Smith, singer
13. Mother Jones, humanitarian
14. Louisa May Alcott, author or novelist
15. Madame C.J. Walker, entrepreneur

First Ladies' First Names (page 59)

1. Martha
2. Abigail
3. Dolley
4. Sarah
5. Abigail
6. Mary
7. Julia
8. Florence, "Flossie"
9. Grace
10. Eleanor
11. Elizabeth, "Bess"
12. Mamie
13. Jacqueline
14. Claudia, "Lady Bird"
15. Thelma
16. Elizabeth, "Betty"
17. Rosalyn
18. Nancy
19. Barbara
20. Hillary

Bonus: Lady Bird Johnson, Pat Nixon

Assassinated Presidents (page 60)

1. Presidents who have been assassinated
2. Dates of presidential assassinations
3. Vice-presidents who took office after presidential assassinations
4. Assassins
5. Cities where an assassination took place
6. Locations where the assassinations took place
7. Home states of assassinated presidents
8. Widowed first ladies

Categories (page 61)

I. 1. Andrew Johnson, Lyndon Johnson
2. John Adams, John Quincy Adams
3. Theodore Roosevelt, Franklin Roosevelt
4. William Henry Harrison, Benjamin Harrison

ANSWER KEY (cont.)

Categories (cont.)

II. 5. Polk   7. Bush
     6. Taft   8. Ford
III. 9. John Adams
    10. John Quincy Adams
    11. Chester Arthur
    12. Dwight Eisenhower
IV. 13. Woodrow Wilson
    14. Calvin Coolidge
    15. Herbert Hoover
    16. Ronald Reagan

Challenge Questions:
Eisenhower
Franklin Roosevelt

Picture Puzzle (page 62)
Answers will vary.

Chain of State Names (page 63)
1. Utah
2. Hawaii
3. Idaho
4. Ohio
5. Oregon
6. New York
7. Kansas
8. South Carolina
9. Alaska
10. Arizona or Alabama
11. Arkansas
12. South Dakota

Numbers of Letters (page 64)
I. 1. Connecticut
    2. Hawaii
    3. Illinois
    4. Minnesota
    5. Missouri
    6. Pennsylvania
II. 7. Massachusetts
III. 8. Mississippi
    9. Tennessee
IV. Answers will vary.

Presidential Hopefuls (page 65)
I. 1992 election
   1. billionaire
   2. jobs
   3. federal
   4. party

Answer: Ross Perot
II. 1996 election
    1. Republican
    2. national
    3. Liddy
Answer: Bob Dole

War Dates (page 66)
1861 + 1812 − 1775 + 1941 − 1917 + 1990 − 1964 − 3 = 1945
1. 12/7/41
2. 2/19/45
3. 6/6/44
4. 1/27/45
5. 8/14/45

Famous American Firsts (pages 67–68)
I. 1. Amelia Earhart
    2. Sandra Day O'Connor
    3. Dr. Sally Ride
    4. John Adams
    5. Neil Armstrong
II. 6. Thanksgiving
    7. rubber
    8. sewing machine
    9. telephone
    10. computer
III. 11. 1587
    12. 1927
    13. 1962
    14. 1860
    15. 1958
IV. 16. Boston, Massachusetts
    17. Delaware
    18. Yellowstone
    19. Chicago, Illinois
    20. Des Plaines, Illinois

This Land Is Your Land (page 69)
1. Oregon (spelling)
2. Rocky Mountains (place)
3. Appalachian Mountains (place)
4. Nevada (spelling)
5. Arizona (spelling)
6. Grand Canyon (place)
7. Rio Grande (place)
8. Mississippi R. (place)
9. Minnesota (spelling)
10. Missouri (spelling)
11. Arkansas (spelling)
12. Mississippi (spelling)
13. Tennessee (spelling)
14. Pennsylvania (spelling)
15. Virginia (spelling)
16. Connecticut (spelling)

Places of Historic Importance (page 70)
1. Jefferson Memorial; Washington, D.C.
2. Lincoln Memorial; Washington, D.C.
3. Mount Rushmore; Black Hills, South Dakota
4. Statue of Liberty; New York, New York
5. George Washington Carver National Monument; Diamond, Missouri
6. Washington Memorial; Washington, D.C.
7. White House; Washington, D.C.
8. Martin Luther King, Jr., Historic Site; Atlanta, Georgia
9. Tomb of the Unknown Soldier; Washington, D.C.
10. Thomas Alva Edison Memorial Tower and Museum; Menlo Park, New Jersey

License Plate Decoder (page 71)
1. Two Explorers
2. U.S. President
3. First Lady
4. Fly Brothers
5. Car Maker
6. Great Leader
7. World War General
8. Indian Chief
9. Inventor
10. Go for the Gold
11. American Indian
12. Mountain Man
Bonus: Answers will vary.

National Symbols (page 72)
1. flag
2. Liberty Bell
3. elephant
4. donkey
5. Great Seal
6. bald eagle
7. Uncle Sam
8. buffalo
9. Mayflower
10. Statue of Liberty

Analogies (page 73)
1. children
2. bus boycott
3. civil rights
4. Supreme Court
5. Rosa Parks
6. Samuel Gompers
7. Panama Canal
8. Martin Luther King, Jr. (suggested answer)
9. Abraham Lincoln
10. Crispus Attucks
11. Benjamin Franklin
12. Pennsylvania
13. American Revolution
14. Bleeding Kansas

Trivia (page 74)
1. The Constitution
2. Neil Armstrong
3. Ben Franklin, Sacajawea, Susan B. Anthony
4. Maine
5. Five rows of six stars and four rows of five stars
6. New York City and Philadelphia
7. 555 feet, 5 1/8 inches
8. Francis Scott Key
9. her right
10. none (It is a district.)
11. a republic or democracy
12. E Pluribus Unum
13. Rhode Island
14. Samuel Langley
15. John Wilkes Booth

People in Pictures (page 75)
1. George Bush
2. Jimmy Carter
3. Ulysses S. Grant
4. Harriet Tubman
5. Davey Crockett
6. Powhatan
7. Booker T. Washington
8. Christopher Columbus
9. Charles Cornwallis